PEATLANDS

Pedro Serrano
PEATLANDS

Translated by
Anna Crowe

Introduced by
W. N. Herbert

PUBLICATIONS
2014

Published by Arc Publications,
Nanholme Mill, Shaw Wood Road
Todmorden OL14 6DA, UK

978 1906570 85 9 (pbk)
978 1906570 86 6 (hbk)

Design by Tony Ward
Printed in Great Britain by T.J. International Ltd, Padstow, Cornwall

ACKNOWLEDGEMENTS
The publishers are grateful to the editors of the following
magazines in which these translated poems have appeared:
'Schoolchildren on Via Augusta' and 'Port', *The Rialto*
(Spring 2009); 'Rodin's Garden', 'Swallows' and 'The Cove at
Aiguafreda', *Boulevard Magenta* (Irish Museum of Modern Art,
2009, issue 4); 'Swallows' *Modern Poetry in Translation* (Third
series, no. 10); 'Feet', 'Snake', 'Inside the Chapel', 'Lustral',
'Swallows' and 'Regent's Canal', *Mexican Poetry Today, 20 / 30
Voices* ed. Brandel France de Bravo (2010).
A separate translation of 'Three Lunatic Songs' was published
in a *partiuta* edition by the Mexican composer Hilda Paredes.
The music is for counter-tenor and string quartet, and was first
performed at the Wigmore Hall, London, and in Paris, in 2011.

Cover photograph: © Pia Elizondo, 2014,
by kind permission of the photographer

Esta publicación fue realizada con el estímulo del
Programa de Apoyo a la Traducción (PROTRAD)
dependiente de instituciones culturales mexicanas.

This publication was made possible with the help
of the Translation Support Program (PROTRAD),
under the auspices of Mexican cultural institutions.

Supported using public funding by
ARTS COUNCIL
LOTTERY FUNDED   ENGLAND

Arc Publications 'Visible Poets' series
Series Editor: Jean Boase-Beier

CONTENTS

The 'Visible Poets' series was established in 2000, and set out to challenge the view that translated poetry could or should be read without regard to the process of translation it had undergone. Since then, things have moved on. Today there is more translated poetry available and more debate on its nature, its status, and its relation to its original. We know that translated poetry is neither English poetry that has mysteriously arisen from a hidden foreign source, nor is it foreign poetry that has silently rewritten itself in English. We are more aware that translation lies at the heart of all our cultural exchange; without it, we must remain artistically and intellectually insular.

One of the aims of the series was, and still is, to enrich our poetry with the very best work that has appeared elsewhere in the world. And the poetry-reading public is now more aware than it was at the start of this century that translation cannot simply be done by anyone with two languages. The translation of poetry is a creative act, and translated poetry stands or falls on the strength of the poet-translator's art. For this reason 'Visible Poets' publishes only the work of the best translators, and gives each of them space, in a Preface, to talk about the trials and pleasures of their work.

From the start, 'Visible Poets' books have been bilingual. Many readers will not speak the languages of the original poetry but they, too, are invited to compare the look and shape of the English poems with the originals. Those who can are encouraged to read both. Translation and original are presented side-by-side because translations do not displace the originals; they shed new light on them and are in turn themselves illuminated by the presence of their source poems. By drawing the readers' attention to the act of translation itself, it is the aim of these books to make the work of both the original poets and their translators more visible.

Jean Boase-Beier

When Pedro Serrano was invited to read his work at StAnza, Scotland's International Poetry Festival, in 2005, I had the task of providing English translations of about ten of his poems. Many of these were taken from his most recent but unpublished collection, *Ronda del Mig* (this is the name of a circular road that runs round the centre of Barcelona – Serrano had been invited to teach for a few years at one of the city's universities). Working on this handful of poems, I was struck both by the lyricism and complexity of the language, and the compelling quality of the voice which was like nothing I had ever read before: they were humane, rich and mysterious poems and I knew then that I wanted to try to translate much more of his work so that English readers could come to know and appreciate it. Pedro sent me a copy of *Desplazamientos* (Candaya, Barcelona 2006) – the volume of selected poems which draws on all the collections, published and unpublished, after 1986. I knew that it would be a challenge. I am not of that school of translators that seek to hitch a ride on the original and create something quite different of their own making. I believe in staying as close as possible to the voice and spirit of the orginal, listening for a tone of voice, being alert to nuances and ambiguities, to the echoes that float up from other places, listening to the poem as a piece of music, as well as a complex weaving of thoughts and images. Fortunately, English is a language rich in synonyms, with a Latinate voice and an Anglo-Saxon voice, and well-able to match the mellifluous qualities of Spanish.

I think that what the reader of Pedro Serrano's poetry first becomes aware of is a most amazing eye at work: each poem unfolds through a highly-focused, loving attention, in language that is both precise and ardent, whether the subject is the moon, a dingy London canal, the human body, lovemaking, feet, stones on a beach, an Italian landscape, or the movement of small children coming out of school. The image of the gaze is central to his work, the gaze but also the sense of touch. For him, days are like windows, and in his later poetry, his passionate gaze observes and often touches the natural

9

world of snake, swallow, lizard, snail, valleys and skyscapes, trees and dung-beetles. In 'The Water That We Drink' (p. 25), from *Fear*, the poet's gaze embraces his family after the death of his sister – a loving gaze that is both calm and concerned, that looks and does not judge, assuaging fear and providing an acceptance of things as they are. His poetry faces up to chaos and accepts it, searching with the exile's longing for the origin of things, the place where objects, bodies and words come together. In his poems, Serrano often links objects subliminally through a succession of vowel sounds, and in these translations I have sought to replicate this.

Likewise from *Fear*, 'Dry Rain' (p. 27) finds chaos even in the act of creation: this is a courageous poem about the desolation of spirit that the act of creation – in this case writing – brings. Its opening lines admit that

> At times the poem is a collapse,
> a slow and painful landslide,
> a dark and scandalous rockfall.

I have tried to reproduce the poet's patterns of assonance in the Spanish with patterns of my own in English, in this case with a series of short *'a'* sounds, as in 'bat'. Writers among us will feel the truth of his description of writing, and feel the force of his imagery: the poet continues by observing that the act of creation, for all its pain and chaos, provides its own healing: "The poem writes itself like a scab" he goes on, and it is precisely in "the striations of soil, / the landmarks and overturned plants, / the fractured dryness in the after-silence," that the poem writes itself. Another poem that is, I think, central to Serrano's poetics is 'The Scribe' (p. 93) and comes from his collection, *Nueces*, which we might translate as 'Kernels'. It opens with a familiar Serranian trope, the image of a man at a window, and I find this a most moving poem, in which we catch the poet surprising himself with how modest and even despised memories can be transformed into something remarkable and beautiful:

Out there the countryside of his childhood shines,
a cradle song, some joke or other.
The evening is red and slow,
his memory is nothing but literary.

And it is out of the débris of childhood – "his old junk,
his shadows" – with their "toilsome couplings and painful
twists", but also their "quiet toughness and their cunning",
that the poet is able to "inherit songs and feathers and bis-
cuits and socks" and make

… from this pain…
an endless reshuffling of opacities and sparkles,
blessed second-hand objects, tales made of glass, knick-knacks,
gold dust his pedlar's trade.

In the opening lines of 'The Scribe' we have seen how,
together with the strength of the gaze, other sense impres-
sions enter and mingle in what is a kind of synaesthesia, and
other examples of this abound and add to the richness of Ser-
rano's language. In 'Regent's Canal' (p. 87) the "flat quack of a
duck trembles in the water"; in the sequence of poems called
'Tuscania' (a small village in the Lazio region of Italy), visual
images merge almost imperceptibly with sounds and silence,
with smells and tactile imagery, to produce a densely inflect-
ed landscape that succeeds in arresting the passing of time (to
which the poet is ever attentive). The poet's gaze homes in on
a skinned rabbit, hanging from a doorway:

the blood is a sweat that oozes through skin,
the body the thin marvel of muscles and nerves.
(p. 77)

Then come echoes of Neruda: "tomato and herbs, / the enticing
aroma of sacrifice", and the poet embraces the idea that this "com-
munal act" – eating – is "savagely human, / appetising and cruel".
  Serrano is a tender love poet, and his poetry exalts bodily
love, while suggesting that love always involves pain of some
kind. One of his most beautiful love poems, arresting in the way

in which the image of the moon and the body of the beloved merge and become one, is 'Lustral' (p. 101). The tone is one of humility, deference, worship, and he places a long adverb, *inmerecidamente* ('undeservedly') – a rare part of speech for Serrano – in key position at the end of the second line. This poem is full of the most astonishing music, and it was both challenging and exhilarating to find musical equivalents in English. Here is one line in Spanish, where the poet uses a series of long *'u'* sounds that reproduce the movement of the swing (the moon is seen as a swing): "El columpio lunar, la rajadura de la luna, la uña de plata." Unable to find long 'u' sounds in English, I have used a series of short *'i'* sounds, seeking to emphasize the thinness of the crescent moon, while still keeping something of the swinging rhythm: "The moon's swing, sliver of moon, fingernail of silver."

The passionate language of this poem is reminiscent of Solomon's *Song of Songs*, and also of 'Noche Oscura' by the Spanish poet and mystic, St. John of the Cross. I have been fortunate in being able to reproduce many of the same sounds as in the Spanish, as here in the tremendous *crescendo* of sound at the end of the poem:

> I crawl on all fours across your body, moon, I ride you,
> moon
> I ride you,
> damp manta-ray,
> mantle of God,
> and mountainous,
> I mount you.

Serrano's love poetry is sometimes reminiscent of Metaphysical poets like Donne, in the way his imagery lends itself to building conceits, and in his poem 'The Sun on Live Coals' (p. 33), he uses cosmic imagery as Donne does. Love-making is described in terms of 'dawning', 'solar harshness', and 'amber sacrifice' and this particular image is just one instance of the motif of preserving and conserving that runs through the book, in images of peat and of fossils. He is a poet who embraces the human body with all its propensity to cause delight and ecstasy, fear and anguish. Indeed, fear is a constant in his poetry, together with oppression, sexual anxiety, despair, dispossession and disintegration. His work fiercely embraces joy and anguish, confronts the one with the other, knows that they are part of the same thing, and reconciles them, which is perhaps why I find his poetry so consoling. He is also a poet with a lovely sense of humour, and 'El arte de fecar' ('The Liminating Art', p. 95) provides a comprehensive, exhortatory yet benevolent study of this despised bodily function. The tone is precise, elegant, reminiscent of the Spanish Baroque poets, and the *frisson* the reader receives comes perhaps from seeing that the poet is taking a taboo subject seriously, treating the body and its difficulties with tenderness and respect, exploring all that can be said about it in highly formal, rhyming language. It was a delight to translate this, to find rhymes and the right tone of voice:

> Shitting is like the art of writing:
> You have to give it thought and just so long
> for everything to come out good and strong.
>
> Sages declare – and they should know –
> that no one ever thinks of suicide
> on the heels of that precise infanticide
>
> and that it scours and rids you of all blame
> and leaves the spirit in an exalted
> sphere of clemency, and cleansed of fault.

He is equally moving on the much overlooked subject of feet in his poem of that name (p. 105). In the opening lines I have created a pattern of short '*e*' sounds to replicate the same vowels in the Spanish:

> Feet clench, make themselves small, run away,
> creasing their wretchedness and fear in lines
> identical to those on our palms and different.

"Feet are extensions of God" he writes, ("which is why they are low down",) and – memorably – feet "are like startled crayfish". Serrano is an acute observer of the natural world, and his poem 'Swallows' (p. 111) has been widely anthologized. The opening lines lay down patterns of vowel sounds, short *'a'*s as in 'bat', *'i'* and long *'u'* ('oo' as in 'food'), that paint a picture of swallows at rest and in motion, and I have sought to replicate this:

> Pinned to the wire like clothes-pegs,
> diminutive seagulls made of wood,
> lithe and tiny in the brutal force of the blue.

I had the pleasure of providing a *partitura* translation of Serrano's 'Three Lunatic Songs' (p. 45), at the request of the Mexican composer, Hilda Paredes, and the music, for counter-tenor and string quartet, was performed in London at the Wigmore Hall in 2011 (the translation in this book is not the *partitura* version). This is an astonishing poem sequence in which the moon acquires a wild, unpredictable personality, "in rut, and adrift", causing destruction and drownings, and the "poor moonstruck souls" to be "always cabined on days like these, / pent with huge heavy padlocks". In the third poem of the sequence I was delighted to be able to find end-rhymes, as well as internal rhymes, to suggest, as far as possible, the spirited, wilful music of the Spanish:

> The moon walks out encumbered
> with so much presence
> she does not remember.
>
> The moon walks out so rounded
> it would be a miracle
> she did not founder.
>
> The moon is unloosed and, yellow,
> dancing, the moon is
> alone in the meadow.

When Pedro and I were thinking about a title for this collection, I felt very strongly that it was important to keep the image of peat, which is present in *Turba* (Peat), one of the books upon which *Desplazamientos* draws. As I have suggested, other motifs, of amber and fossils, are also present in these poems, and it seemed that the preserving properties of peat were an excellent metaphor for the way poetry preserves and transforms experience – and provides fuel to warm the heart. I am delighted that it is Arc Publications, with their superb track record of publishing poetry in translation, and in parallel text, to whom the honour has fallen, and I hope that its readers will love these rich, mysterious and life-affirming poems as much as I do.

Anna Crowe

Pedro Serrano is one of poetry's great natural ambassadors, moving on the one hand between cultures, whether between his native Mexico and Spain, or between the Spanish-speaking world and the Anglo-Saxon; and on the other between the physical world and the human. The debatable territory between consciousness and instinct, and between landscape and animal (including the human animal), is one of his core concerns. As he says in 'The Cove at Aiguafreda' (p. 117):

> Shrinking, we came up against the pebble's roughness,
> a wall from which the sandstone's rubbed away,
> the outline of ourselves.
> Faults and fissures of mineral accretions, that's what we are.

I first knew of him as editor and translator of the anthology produced by him and Carlos López Beltran, *La generación del cordero* (Trilce, 2000), which brought my generation of poets into Spanish for the first time. I first met him in person when he was living in Barcelona in 2004, when his wife was there on diplomatic work, and he acted as host and dragoman, introducing me to the poets of that city, the dead as much as the living.

Here, in an irony he would appreciate, I must confess to misremembering the Catalan restaurant he took us to for my own mythopoeic purposes – I lost the notes I made, and determined that it was the Casa Leopoldo, favourite haunt of Manuel Vázquez Montalbán, after whom Camilleri named his famous Sicilian detective. Somehow I never quite got round to asking him whether I'm right or, more likely, wrong.* (As he says in 'Drawing the Boundary', "The fact is, I do not believe in myself".)

Both as editor and as *littérateur*, the generous inclusivity of his imagination shone out then, and does so now with striking clarity in this comprehensive selection of his work.

---

* The restaurant was not Casa Leopoldo, which is in the Raval, but the Can Massana in Sarriá, a favourite of Jaime Gil de Biedma, now unfortunately disappeared – *Pedro Serrano*

His poetry shows his twin reflexes, like the contraction and extension of the muscles of the heart: the urge to curiosity and then communication.

Author of half a dozen collections between 1986 and 2009, with another, reflecting his time in Barcelona, represented here but still to be published, he has a pronounced gift for the musicality of Spanish, as evinced by his interest in libretto. His poetry has demarked its own distinctive territory from the outset – indeed it is about territories, both invoking and, especially, embodying them: the body becomes a kind of geography, and its passions and functions are seen almost as species of weather. As he states in a passage that seems at the heart of his poetics:

Trade winds pass over the chest, swim blue over the hands, pass.
Fear returns, re-establishes itself in the ungodliness of the waist,
you have to go back to the source of the pain, make it
    become dream,
pounce in the act of flight, decontract.
Its breath grows before my eyes like pasture,
sex's sweet black majesty, its crammed and sweaty pubis,
the open presence that I penetrate.
From my centre the wrong windows shatter, grow still.
An immaterial melting makes the flesh flesh,
stone is crushed, becoming sand.
To enter is to come to one's own centre, a flowing wisdom.

(p. 75)

A marvellous love poet, though, as this example indicates, one concerned with relationship in the metaphysical as much as the sexual or familial senses, he tends less toward the poetry of disrupted social contract and political tension that we find in a Latin American contemporary like, say, the Argentinian poet Joaquín O. Giannuzzi, and more to the atavistic impulse we recall in the Neruda of 'Too Many Names':

When I lived among the roots
they pleased me more than flowers did,
and when I spoke to a stone
it rang like a bell.

This is not to say there is an avoidance of the violence that we as humans are so ingenious at – in one of his more stunning images (and one which has a neatness and elaboration we would associate with the Metaphysical poets, but which in the Spanish tradition perhaps derives equally from Surrealism and from Góngora), he compares the turning Earth to a revolver:

We are a chamber in darkness,
the globe a revolver.
The world is night and we are there inside it,
loaded and expectant bullets.

(p. 89)

It would however be more accurate to observe that in his work, as Blake asserts, everything that lives is holy, and each human function is as appropriate as another for the purposes of poetry. In 'The Liminating Art' (p. 95) – notice how neatly Anna Crowe's translation catches the original 'El Arte de Fecar': the play on 'eliminating' matching precisely that on 'defecar' – Serrano draws on the reductive Catalan tradition of the *caganer* or 'shitter' to draw out a surprisingly elegant comparison between the place of the excreter and the escritoire.

There is as that example suggests a directness to his work despite the elegance of his language, so brilliantly and unerringly matched by these scrupulous translations. He is unafraid of the large gesture, as in "It is cold in the vast and unprotected slaughter-house of the heavens" (from the opening of 'Three Lunatic Songs', p. 45), or of drawing out the interrelation between art (particularly, of course, poetry) and life: "I fold my body into this attentive pen" (p. 69).

In this, he is both a counter and a corrective to the too frequent British assumption that the rhetorical tends only to excess or to artificiality. Forever testing our boundaries, he will turn from a poem about a mermaid to one about a saleswoman with a sense that the juxtaposition, the disjunction, is part of the point.

The intention throughout his work appears to be nothing less than visionary: to transform us through language, compelling us to rethink, re-imagine and re-envision the world and our place in it; and to break down our unconsidered assumptions about opposed categories like thought and feeling, human and animal, by continually returning us to the matrix of the body – "To enter is to come to one's own centre, a flowing wisdom".

There is in this something at once Quixotic and compelling. What we make of the world, he suggests, is ourselves, at once a fiction and the only meaningful gesture. At its finest, Pedro Serrano's poetry is both completely involving and seemingly inevitable, and in its aspiration to be an act as well as a force of nature, we find ourselves challenged and marvellously reconfigured.

W. N. Herbert

PEATLANDS

"The high fields of scree are solidified waves of stone, long swells of unmoving time. Tall trees, once whispering in the wind, have sunk into peat bogs, where time ferments in the marshy pools. Here and there, flowering woodland penetrates the darkness of the firs and the sea of stones, forming wedges of broad-leaved trees, fragrant night-flowering plants and humming frail-winged insects. There, the noble tree sings."

KERSTIN EKMANN
translated by Anna Paterson

I

de **EL MIEDO**

DIBUJO DE LAS COSAS

Las cuatro. Alguien pasa corriendo por la calle
La música y la soledad de esta tarde
que empieza a oscurecer.
La ventana.
Un árbol ya sin hojas en que inicia el invierno.
La calma y las chimeneas en la casa de enfrente.
El cielo, pesadamente gris, abandonando el día.
El cigarro que consume la música y la tarde y el poema.
Una manzana en el frutero.
La dama de Shalott en la pared.
Unos helechos secos de los fríos de Gales. Una muñeca.
El secreto y perdurable estar de las cosas,
en su reposo,
en su lento ir aconteciendo cada día,
en la mirada que ponen en mí,
en el callado poema que depositan.

I

from **FEAR**

SKETCH OF THINGS

Four o'clock. Someone runs past along the street.
The music and solitude of afternoon
which is starting to darken.
The window.
A tree already without leaves where winter begins.
The calm and the chimneys of the house opposite.
The sky, heavily grey, abandoning the day.
The cigarette which consumes the music and the afternoon
    and the poem.
An apple in the fruit bowl.
The Lady of Shalott on the wall.
Some ferns, withered by the chills of Wales. A doll.
The secret and enduring nature of things,
in their repose,
in the slow way they go on happening each day,
in the gaze they bestow on me,
in the hushed poem that they lay down.

EL AGUA QUE BEBEMOS

Mi hermano al otro lado de la sala.
Pasamos.
Somos todos nosotros dolor acumulado.

Tocamos las vidas que nos hacen,
heridas de los otros,
una mirada,
una plática que se forma,
una caricia o la tristeza de mi padre.

Algunos azares ya sabidos nos obligaron a vivir
la misma casa, la misma mesa, las mismas obsesiones.
Amor entretejido,
cada uno ha ido haciéndolo reposar en su historia
de muy distinto modo.
Así la hermana muerta, su larga enfermedad, su paz
    profunda,
esa incierta mirada que nos cerca.
Querer es una forma de extrañar
y a veces es difícil en el tacto continuo.
Pienso sus gestos, su manera
tan personal de ser, sus diferencias.
Alguna vez
en el raro mar de la costumbre
hemos quebrado el arco de distancias.

Por eso puedo ahora escribir estas cosas.

THE WATER THAT WE DRINK

My brother on the other side of the room.
Things happening.
We are all a slow piling up of sorrow.

We touch those lives that make us,
wounds of others,
a glance,
a conversation that takes shape,
a caress or my father's sadness.

Certain accidents already known obliged us to live
in the same house, at the same table, the same obsessions.
Love interwoven,
each of us has gone on making it settle into his own story
in very distinct ways.
Thus this dead sister, her long illness, her deep calm,
that vague glance searching for us.
Loving is a way of missing someone
and at times it is difficult with this daily contact.
I think their expressions, their very personal manner
of being, their differences.
At some time
in the strange sea of custom
we have broken the bow of distances.

That is why I can now write these things.

LA LLUVIA SECA

A veces el poema es un derrumbe,
un lento y doloroso desprendimiento,
una oscura y escandalosa caída de piedras.
Como una lluvia seca
la cascada de rocas se despedaza
no en el aire sino dentro de sí misma
y el poema es ese polvo de piedra amontonada,
ese duro esqueleto de la lluvia
en donde apenas puede respirarse.
El poema se graba como costra:
no es aquel lento movimiento de ola,
polvo de espuma sobre la caída,
lento despedazarse de las cosas.
Es las estrías de tierra,
los mojones y plantas revolcadas,
la rota sequedad en el silencio posterior,
el hueco desolado en la pared descubierta.
El poema es la costra,
la imagen al final despedazada,
la ruina de esa imagen.

DRY RAIN

At times the poem is a collapse,
a slow and painful landslide,
a dark and scandalous rockfall.
Like dry rain
the tumbled rocks fragment
not in the air but within,
and the poem is that pile of stony dust,
that hard skeleton of rain
in which you can barely breathe.
The poem writes itself like a scab:
it is not that slow, wave-like motion,
dusting of foam on the downfall,
slow breaking-into-pieces of things.
It is the striations of soil,
the landmarks and overturned plants,
the fractured dryness in the after-silence,
the woeful hole in the stripped wall.
The poem is the scab,
the image finally broken in pieces,
the ruins of that image.

RECONSTRUCCIÓN

En el espejismo de las horas
se inventa la conciencia de lo vano.
Miro, y las imágenes que el tiempo me permite
no perdonan, no forman.
Son el necio esqueleto de la certeza
que como la acojinada palabra del farsante
luego de las aguas y de los gestos,
en el agotado lecho del tiempo que fue río
fósil de caracol piedra se vuelve.

(Las luces y las aguas y los gestos.
La rítmica corriente de las conversaciones,
la sal, los deslizamientos y las dudas.)

En el azar y la mirada el alma se levanta
y la memoria toca ahora los fósiles quebrados,
las verdades, las dolorosas puntas del vacío.

REBUILDING

In the mirage of the hours
the awareness of what is futile is concocted.
I stare, and the images which time allows me
do not forgive, do not take shape.
They are the stubborn skeleton of certitude
which like the fraud's cushioned word
immediately after the waters and the gestures,
in the dried-up bed of time that was once a river
turns into a fossilized snail of stone.

(The lights and the waters and the gestures.
The rhythmic current of conversations,
the salt, the landslides and the doubts.)

Through chance and the gaze the spirit rises up
and memory now touches the broken fossils,
truths, painful thorns of emptiness.

DESECACIÓN

En la escisión de la columna
una mirada y una sonrisa
despedazándome entre ceja y ceja.

En ese amor, línea de sal, aguafuerte,
se me rompen los huesos y me doblo
y me doblo
como el cangrejo se deshace
a la orilla del mar
llena de sol
la descarnada cáscara sin carne.

DESICCATION

In the splitting of the spine
a glance and a smile
cleaving me between eyebrow and eyebrow.

In this love, salt-line, etching,
my bones break and I buckle
and I buckle
like the crab coming apart
on the sea-shore
brimful of sun
the bare shell emptied of flesh.

EL SOL EN ASCUAS

Y no son nada
las palabras viejas y las nuevas
en el vuelco de imágenes continuo
amanecer tensado
desde tu piel alada adivinada
como collar de caracoles descolgándose
en el rigor solar de la caída
en las continuas olas del deseo
tacto hacia el tacto
en el incendio anhelo de los cuerpos
hasta el largo puntal envenenado
dulce
del ámbar sacrificio
dual.

THE SUN ON LIVE COALS

Nor are they nothing
the old words and the new
in the unending astonishments of images
dawning made taut
from your winged skin guessed-at
like a necklace of shells coming down
in the solar harshness of the fall
in the continuous waves of desire
touch towards touch
in the breath blaze of our bodies
as far as the long, poisoned beam
and sweet
with the amber sacrifice
of the pair of us.

LA FUERZA

He reunido tus ojos
y he seguido el retorno de tus cejas
y la pregunta grave de tu sonrisa.

Hasta dónde podremos, oh, mi amiga,
desmadejar la vida
para seguir a tientas el misterio y el amor.

Porque aunque a veces vuela mi sonrisa
la efigie de tu voz,
hueco del beso,
el desamor a veces abre y luce mis piernas
y la desgana
opaca llena la curva de mi mano.

Amiga, dulce amiga,
formas despacio el arco de la vida.

STRENGTH

I have assembled your eyes
and I have followed the return your eyebrows make
and your smile's serious question.

As far as where we'll be able, oh my sweetheart,
to make life simpler
in order to follow gropingly after mystery and love.

Because although my smile sometimes flies beside
and alights upon the effigy of your voice,
kissing's hollow nest,
indifference sometimes opens and lights up my legs
and dense reluctance
fills the curve of my hand.

Sweetheart, dearest love,
slowly you fashion life's rainbow.

II

de IGNORANCIA

LA SIRENA

Soy ese grito.
He llamado a los hombres y me han seguido.

En este falso cuerpo que aparento creyeron que tocaban
todos sus sueños y todo su destino.
Así era, así fue de algún modo.

Mi hablar y mis palabras son una música y un llamado
melodiosos,
nada cuentan.
Como el rumor helado de las corrientes
y su profundidad oscura e insensata. Nada cuentan.

Tengo la suave calma inmemorial de los peces,
su lustroso cuerpo sin vestigio y sin sexo,
su persistencia lenta y tensa,
su invulnerabilidad.

Me ha sido negado el ser mujer
pero es mi llamado que esta impotencia engasta,
el lamento largo y continuo de mi canto,
mi ingrata seducción.

He oído tantos gritos,
tantos ahogados que derraman su sueño,
tantos naufragios e ilusiones.

No sé por qué sigo parada en esta piedra,
esperando, esperando…

Mis verdes ojos brillan intensos
e indescifrables.

Sólo la eternidad dura del mar, y me acompaña.

II
from IGNORANCE

THE MERMAID

I am that cry.
I have called to men and they have followed me.

With this false body I put on they believed they fingered
all their dreams and all their future.
So it was, so it was, in a way.

My speech and my words are a music and a summons
melodious,
saying nothing.
Like the currents' icy murmur
and their dark and senseless deeps. Saying nothing.

The smooth and immemorial calm of fish is mine,
their sexless, lustrous body that leaves no footprint,
their slow and tense persistence,
their invulnerability.

Being a woman has been denied me
but this impotence is the setting for my call,
my singing's long, continual lament,
my thankless seduction.

I have heard so many cries,
so many drowned who pour out all their dream,
so many shipwrecks and illusions.

I don't know why I stay here on this rock,
waiting, waiting...

My green eyes shine, intense,
undecipherable.

Only the endless sea endures, and comes along with me.

LA VENDEDORA

Una escalera eléctrica
lleva esas pedacerías de cartón
con pelos y con uñas.

La indiferencia huele a fotocopia
y mantequilla rancia.

Hay una solapada ruindad en todos los objetos, la gente.

En mis dedos queda su terrosa condición,
el deterioro neutro del comercio y el polvo.

En la taza del día el café se hace nata,
las puertas se abren y se cierran,
el cenicero es un charco en el que chapaleo.

SALESWOMAN

An escalator
carries away these bits of cardboard
along with hairs and nails.

Indifference smells of photocopier
and rancid butter.

There's a sly meanness about things and people.

Their earthy nature sticks to my fingers,
the sexless wear and tear of trade and dust.

In the day's cup coffee grows a skin,
doors open and close,
the ashtray is a puddle I splash about in.

LA CONDENA

La oscuridad es el centro de toda historia.
El tiempo y el momento se detienen allí,
allí se cimbran y se cierran.

Ah, si todo se quedara como está,
el florero en la mesa y las flores apenas,
el reloj desprendido de su hermetismo,
abandonado todo en su quietud, en su temblor,
en su estancia redonda y sin flujo.

Ah, si uno pudiera detenerse así,
si uno pudiera ser en ese acto
su propio cáliz, su patena.

Si uno pudiera quedarse aquí con uno mismo,
en el instante,
como una ola inundada en la luz azul que la alimenta,
en el ansia anhelante de la espuma,
en su cresta.

Pero las cosas fluyen, desencadenan, sentencian.

THE SENTENCE

Darkness is at the kernel of every history.
Time and the moment linger there,
swing there then close.

Ah, if things would only stay as they are,
the vase on the table and the flowers barely,
the clock deprived of its secrecy,
everything abandoned to its quiet, its trembling,
its rounded state, without flux.

Ah, if one could only linger thus,
if one could only in this action be
one's own chalice, own paten.

If one could only remain here with oneself,
in the moment,
like a wave flooding in the blue light that nourishes it,
in the foam's panting anguish,
on its crest.

But things flow, unravel, pass sentence.

Hojas, árboles ateridos como espantos y gritos, soledades,
multitud de corrientes en las que forman su realidad,
chamuscados ramales.
Un mar acumulado de distintas hebras o mechones de sal y espuma,
un sordo amontonarse en las esquinas y sótanos y rincones,
como si en ellos hubiera miedo, como si sintieran,
como si su rumor fuera un llanto, o un hijo o un rezo.
Mezcladas como culpas o pesadillas van hojas de periódico arrugadas,
bolsas de papas fritas, celofanes, algunas varas.
Toda esa indiferencia que es la ciudad allí se muestra:
el lento pasto circular de su océano,
su frenesí de harina, su masa espesa,
la densidad de grumos y de yemas.
Y allí van siendo pisadas cáscaras y recuerdos, ruidos,
chapoteos,
manchas de aceite y de basura, pájaros muertos y pescados,
rastros del turbio movimiento de la renovación y las mareas.

LEAVES, SECOND DWELLING

Leaves, numb trees like frights and cries, loneliness,
a multitude of currents in which their reality takes shape,
scorched boughs.
A heaped-up sea of different threads or wisps of salt and foam,
a muffled piling-up in nooks and corners and basements,
as though there were fear in them, as though they could feel,
as though their murmur were weeping, or a child or a prayer.
Mixed in like faults or nightmares run crumpled pages of newspapers,
chip bags, cellophane, a few twigs.
All this indifference that is the city is revealed there:
the slow circular plankton of its ocean,
its frenzy of flour, its thick dough,
the density of curds and yolks.
And there endlessly trodden underfoot are shells and memories, sounds,
splashes,
stains from oil and refuse, dead birds and fish,
remains of the cloudy movement of renewal and tides.

TRES CANCIONES LUNÁTICAS

I

Hace frío en la vasta y desabrigada carnicería del cielo,
un sufrimiento ausente y desprotegido,
el peso enorme de nubes y de ráfagas,
hecho jirones el paisaje asolado,
hecho jirones, a campotraviesa.

Por los desabrigados campos,
el baile todo de sargazos y voces excluidas,
ahogos y murmullos del ahogo.

En el pantano negro y estancado que no refleja nada,
desierto y aterido como pálido piso que nadie viera,
que nadie recorriera paso a paso,
en un desliz sobre ese mármol negro,
sin una voz, sin una condolencia,
pasa la luna,
inquieta.

Como una incandescencia la luna mira,
como un encantamiento la luna manda,
como una inusitada cenicienta huye la luna.

Ronda el viento, ronda el hado.

La noche fija sus atónitos ojos azulados en tanto cielo extenso.
Allá, tan lejos, la luna vaga en brama, a la deriva.

A su merced las aguas y la vida.

THREE LUNATIC SONGS

I

It is cold in the vast and unprotected slaughter-house of the heavens,
a suffering that is remote and without defences,
the enormous weight of clouds, of squalls and gales,
torn into tatters a landscape laid waste,
torn into tatters across the country.

Over the unprotected fields,
the dance is all of kelp and seaweed and of excluded voices,
of drownings and murmurings of drowning.

Out in the marsh that's black and still and stagnant, where nothing
    is reflected,
deserted and benumbed like a pallid cloth that no one may see,
that no one will wander over step by footstep,
in a slithering slide across that black marble,
without any voice, or any condolence,
the moon passes by,
uneasy.

Like an incandescence the moon is staring,
like an enchantment the moon holds sway,
like an unwonted Cinderella the moon runs away.
The wind is patrolling, fate is patrolling.

The night stares with bluish, astonished eyes at so great a span of sky.

Away, far off, the moon goes wandering, in rut, and adrift.

At her mercy the waters and life.

II

A los lunáticos
hay que encerrarlos siempre en estos días,
los candados que pesen y ni un solo visillo para la luz lunar alucinante,
a los lunáticos,
que el corazón les come el alma en estas noches,
aunque haya nubes,
aunque haya cielo bajo y enterrado, encapotado en sí, a los lunáticos
hay que vaciarles ojos y lengua para que no se ahoguen y se
hundan,
para que no
se vayan
como una láctea vía que fuera luz y huella,
como si la saliva les huyera,
como si ellos en ella fueran y en esa vista despavorida,
a los lunáticos, ay,
habría que acompañarlos de la mano
para que no se pierdan y se ofusquen,
ay, a los lunáticos.

II

As for poor moonstruck souls
they must be always cabined on days like these,
pent with huge heavy padlocks and not a wisp of curtain whereby
    the moon's illusive light may enter,

and these poor moonstruck ones,
whose heart devours their soul on nights like these,
though it may be cloudy,
though the sky may lower, come close to earth, be buried, all
    cloaked and overcast, these wretched moonstruck souls
must have their eyes gouged, tongue torn out of them, so that
    they're neither drowned nor confounded,
so that they don't
go wandering
just like a milky way that's source of light and footprint,
as though their own saliva fled their mouth,
just as though they were there inside her, and in that fearsome
    and eerie vista,
and these poor moonstruck ones, ah,
we need to hold their hand when they go walking
so that they don't get lost, nor yet be blinded,
ah, these poor moonstruck souls.

alas, the poor moonstruck.

III

La luna va tan ella
consigo misma
que no se acuerda.

La luna va redonda,
sería una suerte
que no se hunda.

La luna se ha soltado,
baila la luna
sola en el prado.

III

The moon walks out encumbered
with so much presence
she does not remember.

The moon walks out so rounded
it would be a miracle
she did not founder.

The moon is unloosed and, yellow,
dancing, the moon is
alone in the meadow.

CONFIANZA DEL VIENTO

I

La oí lejos, lejos, como una espada azul de medianoche,
como un filo que creciera desde la punta helada de sus labios,
como un cuchillo de agua que en su estridencia no se oyera.
Yo pensé que era un bulto y que gemía en su propio vacío,
¡perdonadme!,
yo pensé que esa caída era digna de un traje sin nadie que lo llene,
yo pensé que todo era falso, perdonadme,
y que nosotros éramos fantasmas.
Así caminé entonces por el mar en la tarde y era invierno,
y era la playa larga y pedregosa y el tiempo duro y acerado.
Era todo un grito y un pájaro se ocultó entre los riscos,
en su candor mirándonos despiertos, en su candor mirándolo
    nosotros.
Porque éramos dos o éramos tres los que allí estábamos
e hicimos el amor como si el tiempo fuera el cielo y nosotros
    ángeles
y aullábamos y huíamos como la piel en ascuas y el gris veteado
    de la tarde,
como un vestido a rayas negras y perla que le cayera a ella por la
    espalda,
porque ellos tocaban cada punta y el mar era ya verde,
y se abrían en el alma hasta la entrega,
y allí eran puros como el aliento mineral y la madrugada,
y el mar era invernal y encapotado.

THE WIND'S TRUST

I

I heard her afar off, like a blue sword of midnight,
like an edge that grew from the frozen point of her lips,
like a knife made of water that in its stridency could not be heard.
I thought it was a shape and that it moaned in its own voice,
forgive me!
I thought that this cadence was worthy of a suit of clothes with no
    one to fill it,
I thought it was all fake, forgive me,
and that we ourselves were ghosts.
And so I walked then by the sea in the evening and it was winter,
and the beach was long and stony and the time as hard and sharp
    as steel.
Everything was a shriek and a bird hid itself among the crags,
in its whiteness warily watching us, in its whiteness watching it
    ourselves.
For we were two or else we were three of us there
and we made love as though the weather were heaven and we were
    angels
and we howled and fled as though our skin were live coals and the
    brindled grey of the evening,
like a dress striped with black and pearl that could fall from off
    her back,
for they were touching every edge and the sea was green now,
and they opened up in their souls in sheer surrender,
and they were pure, there, as mineral breath and the first of the day,
and the sea was wintery and overcast.

51

II

Éramos agua y ella era la tierra y allí reverdecíamos,
reencarnábamos,
echaba yemas la primavera y la piel,
echaba yemas el alma por las uñas,
echaba yemas el agua del amor, inerme entre los dedos.
Y era lustrosa en mis manos su piel de yegua,
escurridiza y tensa y azulada su piel de yegua,
azul como la tierra y como el limo su piel de yegua,
asaltadas las venas y las aletas de la nariz abiertas, extendidas,
afanadas en respirar el propio aliento y el otro,
y ella era mía como sus ojos grandes en la entrega,
como mi amor de boca llena,
y el lomo azul del mar era entonces combado y sudoroso.

III

Era el amor la flor que aquellos dos llevaban en la boca,
era el amor redondo como una flor que se machaca entre los labios,
frutal como el temblor enamorado de sus labios, carnal como
    sus labios.
Y era el amor azul como su miedo, masticado y tragado como su
    miedo,
aterido el amor como su nombre.
Hasta que las ansias nos separen, dijeron,
hasta que las ansias lleguen y eleven tanta tierra pavorosa,
hasta que las ansias muerdan el alma lívida y el mar sea ya de piedra
y todo quiebre
y allí desencadenen la furia y el pavor de ser hombre y mujer.
Hasta que las ansias lleguen se dijeron.

II

We were water and she was the earth and there we grew green again,
put on new flesh,
spring and the skin were putting forth leaf buds,
leaf buds put forth by the soul from its nails,
running unarmed through fingers, love's water was putting
    forth leaf buds.
And it shone in my hands, her skin like a mare's,
slippery and taut and tinged with blue, her skin like a mare's,
blue like the earth and like mud, her skin like a mare's,
her veins assailed and her nostrils wide-open,
thirstily gulping her own breath and the other,
and she was mine as her eyes were, huge in surrender,
like my love that filled my mouth,
and the sea's blue back was curved then, and sweating.

III

Love was the flower that those two carried in their mouth,
it was love rounded like the flower that's chewed between the lips,
fruit-bearing like the amorous trembling of her lips, carnal as
    her lips.
And it was love as blue as her fear, chewed and swallowed like
    her fear,
shuddering, this love, just like her name.
Until anguish separate us two, they said,
until anguish come and winnow so much dreadful earth,
until anguish bite the pale spirit and the sea be turned to stone
and everything shatter
and unleash there the fury and dread of being man and woman.
Until anguish come, they told each other.

IV

Ahora yo veo venir la espada como un destino,
yo veo venir su filo lento y su aliento,
soy este destello aviado y este miedo,
soy esa espada que atraviesa sus cuerpos y atraviesa,
en ella yo respiro y la primavera es tal como se dijo,
la primavera es cruel como nosotros.
Aquí vemos venir la muerte dura y el mar y el inútil pasado
    sin movernos.
Aquí la hierba hierve, quema la rabia en esta tierra.
Aquí crece el pavor de mármol de sus venas,
aquí las algas suyas hacen presa de fuerzas y de músculos.
Estamos yertos aquí, aquí vencidos por la espada del miedo.
Y el mar aquí es tormento y es silencio.
Seco es el mar aquí,
como un cristal insomne enmudecido.

IV

Now do I see the sword approach like fate,
I see its slow edge coming and its breath,
I am this ready gleam, this fear,
I am that sword that cuts through its bodies and cuts,
in her I breathe and the spring is just as was told,
the spring is cruel as we are.
Here we watch hard death come and the sea and the
     useless past without stirring.
Here the grass boils, rage burns in this land.
Here grows the marble dread of her veins,
here her seaweed seizes strength and muscles.
We are rigid here, vanquished here by the sword of fear.
And the sea here is this torment and silence.
Dry is the sea here,
like an unsleeping crystal grown dumb.

V

Amanece la playa despojada,
echada encima del mar como cansancio,
de bruces contra el agua que apenas y la toca y la sacude.
Hay sol, y el pedregal de algas desbarata su rigidez de
   restos y de huesos.
Los cueros vuelven a sentir calor, se desentumen,
crujen en el meneo torpe del sol y de la brisa,
estiran su aterida carcasa de cangrejos.
Un vocerío avisa que algo es cierto
y el diablo cobra caro su despertar.
Ve las espadas rotas por el suelo,
ve el mar de nuevo puro,
ve el cielo como un don que fuera de ellos.
El aire huele a hiedra deshilada
y el viento pasa terso sin más señas.
El mar se oye llegar como un respiro,
continuo y repetido como un respiro.

V

The beach dawns, stripped clean,
thrown over the sea like weariness,
fallen headlong against the water which barely touches or
    shakes it.
There is sun, and the seaweedy shingle untangles from its
    rigidity refuse and bones.
Stiff as leather, they start to feel warmth once more, they
    lose their numbness,
they creak in the sluggish sway of the sun and the breeze,
they stretch their numb carcass of crabs.
A clamour warns that something is certain
and the devil charges dearly for their awakening.
He sees the swords lying broken on the ground,
he sees the sea with its purity restored,
he sees the sky like a gift that belongs to them.
The air smells of torn ivy
and the wind passes smoothly with no comment.
The sea can be heard coming in like a breath,
continuous, over and over like a breath.

III

de TURBA

¶

No hay
posesión
sobre las cosas.
La hilera
de este mundo
se deslíe.
El fresno pierde
sus hojas
de arriba abajo.
En las puertas
quedan astillas
mientras la fronda
se contrae.
Se borran
las sombras.
Todo pasa
por las manos
como guasa.
El mundo
se desconoce
y se deforma.

III

from **PEAT**

¶

There is no
ownership
over things.
The yarn
of this world
unravels.
The beech loses
its leaves
from the crown down.
Splinters stay
embedded in doors
while the foliage
withers.
Shadows
are rubbed out.
Like luck
everything slips
through the fingers.
The world
denies itself
and falls apart.

¶

Todo se apelotona como leche cuajada,
como vómito amargo que aventara
pedazos de intestino, semillas, bilis,
lo que se pudo tragar y lo que no.
En la plancha de vidrio quedan los restos,
en la charola de aluminio lo inventariado,
en la piel la ceniza y la electricidad muerta.
Todo lo pasado se mueve ahora como un agua turbia,
como un burro muerto que ahí se pudre
y que otros beben río abajo, desapercibidos.
Todo lo pasado se queda aquí, regurgitando.

¶

Everything coagulates like curdled milk,
like sour vomit that throws up
bits of intestine, seeds, bile,
what could be swallowed and what could not.
On the sheet of glass lie the remains,
on the aluminium tray the detailed account,
on the skin, ash and dead static.
The entire past now moves like cloudy water,
like a dead donkey rotting upstream
and which others drink further down, unaware.
The whole of the past remains here, regurgitating.

¶

El dolor de los dientes,
las encías lastimadas por el movimiento de los ganchos,
el buche de agua y el escupitajo de saliva y sangre,
el derrumbamiento al levantarse.
Coger el vaso de plástico con el líquido azul,
estirarse hacia la palangana,
doblarse y escupir.
Y luego y antes la conciencia,
el temor a los ganchos que se mueven adentro,
tocan los dientes, los raspan, los ejecutan.
Y la tristeza que ese dolor ocupa,
el miedo y el vacío que ese dolor habita.
Abrir la boca y entregarse a esas manos
ajenas que allí hurgan como una confesión.

¶

Toothache,
with gums hurt by the probes' movement,
the mouthful of water and the spitting out of saliva and blood,
collapsing as you try to get up.
Reaching for the plastic cup and its blue liquid,
stretching over towards the basin,
bending and spitting.
And then and beforehand the knowledge,
the fear of the probes that move about inside,
tapping the teeth, scraping them, playing them.
And the sadness that this pain takes up,
the fear and the emptiness that this pain dwells in.
Opening your mouth and surrendering to those alien
hands that jab at what is almost a confession.

¶

Cae el saco oscuro de avispas y juguetes revueltos,
rotos los coches, llenas de tierra las mariposas,
abierto como nido de pandora que oscureciera al mundo,
como un contrarregalo que a quién le sirve.
Sólo hace daño al niño que mueve las piezas,
trata de organizar el descalabro, de ver qué queda,
entre el zumbido horrendo y el mareo.
¿Dónde meter las manos sin que te piquen?

¶

Dark with wasps and jumbled toys the bag drops,
the cars smashed, the butterflies covered in soil,
open like a Pandora's nest that might darken the world,
like an anti-gift of use to who-on-earth.
It harms only the child who moves the pieces,
tries to set the damage to rights, to see what is left,
between the horrendous buzzing and the dizziness.
Where can he put his fingers without being stung?

¶

Una brújula azul sin ningún piso,
una madeja de color de orín,
una desproporción en cuatro huesos,
una seca impresión en las entrañas,
un impotente resquebrajo inmóvil,
la nomenclatura en la mandíbula,
quieta, acerada, necia, rota, erguida,
la nuca nunca que se agita seca,
el sexo lucidor desobediente,
las agujas del ansia en cada palmo.

¶

A blue compass-needle pointing nowhere,
a skein the colour of urine,
a lack of proportion in all four limbs,
a dry feeling in the gut,
an impotent, motionless crack,
the naming on the tip of your tongue,
placid, steely, stubborn, debauched, swollen,
the nape that never trembles, dry,
the brilliant sex unbiddable,
needles of anguish in each palm.

¶

Lo que tengo es la pluma.
Como una raya vil encajonada entre dos paralelas.
El extremo sensible con que la realidad se hace pedazos,
surge, se encamina.
La difamada lanceta ronda la oscuridad,
anda en el desconcierto, afina el punto.
La palabra no choca con su propio sentido.
Es una rabia que respira y que agita,
marea árboles, encontronazos,
una y otra vez en las enredaderas del cuerpo,
en la miseria de las piernas,
en la angustia intransigente del sexo.
Doblo mi cuerpo en esta pluma atenta,
busco una línea que seguir, un gesto,
un balbuceante atropello que organice.
Voy por las palabras como si tallara los músculos en las esquinas.

¶

What I have is the pen.
Like a wretched line boxed between two parallels.
The sensitive tip that the real world hacks to bits
rises up, sets out.
The maligned goad roams the darkness,
makes for trouble, sharpens its point.
The word does not collide with its meaning.
It is a rage that breathes and shakes,
setting trees swirling, collisions,
again and again in the body's tangles,
in the wretchedness of legs,
in sex's implacable anguish.
I fold my body into this attentive pen,
I look for a line to follow, an expression,
a stammering outrage that takes charge.
I travel along words as though carving muscles on corners.

¶

Este es el punto ciego del agua.
En este punto ciego a ciegas llueve,
llueve en el cuerpo el mineral.
Es en el cuerpo donde está,
el aguamala de la miel,
el goteadero de la piel,
la gota de sudor del semental.
Cuatro paredes y azulejos neutros,
la piel reverberante y aterrada,
cobalto de la sed,
esa gota de luz manchada, inane,
polvo en la gelatina, piel
en el hospital de porcelana.
Como si fuera culpa este deseo,
la zafra de ese cuerpo,
la ventosa arenisca,
su despertar.

¶

This is water's blind spot.
At this blind spot it is raining blindly,
mineral raining on to the body.
The body is where it is,
the medusa made of honey,
the drip, drip of the skin,
the stallion's bead of sweat.
Four walls and neutral tiles,
The skin shimmering and appalled,
cobalt of thirst,
that drop of soiled, vacant light,
dust in the jelly, skin
in the china infirmary.
As though it were fault, this desire,
the syrup-harvest of that body,
the sandstone cupping-bowl,
its awakening.

Como un caracol sordo en la medianoche circunspecta,
como un escarabajo que hollara siempre la misma mierda.
Siete años de piedra y apenas prueba,
de raya tras raya tras raya y apenas grava,
de desmesurados sacrificios y nada.
Los objetos se bordan con las manos, los años,
la vida debiera ser como un recorrido de la piel y otro,
la candidez un ritmo que alguna vez pudiera pronunciarse.
Habito un mismo laberinto lleno de huesos y basura,
en cada esquina un calco viejo, destartalado.
un andar olvidadizo y deshecho.
Los cuatro goznes sin carne ni deseo,
un saladero animal que apenas lamen algunas vacas,
un mismo punto impenetrable.
Miro una luz que queda fija sobre el piso,
miro las luces intermitentes que señalan el cambio año con año,
los vastos escenarios de la escasez,
la mala hierba inútil de esta vida.
Quieto en mi piedra lamo las heridas de escarabajo,
masco de los desechos de los días,
rumio mi impotencia y la gota dura del tiempo,
el pie quebrado y la señal de huida.
Como un bicho sin curso me apesadumbro.

¶

Like a deaf snail at cautious midnight,
like a dung-beetle forever treading the same shit.
Seven years of stone and barely anything to show for it,
of line after line after line and barely a scratch,
of inordinate sacrifice and nothing.
Things are embroidered with the hands, the years,
life should be like a journey of the skin and different,
innocence a rhythm we might at some time utter.
I inhabit the same labyrinth full of bones and rubbish,
on every corner an old, dilapidated tracing,
a shambling, absent-minded way of walking.
The four hinges without flesh or desire,
a salt-lick that only a few cows rasp with their tongues,
the same impenetrable point.
I gaze at a light that goes on shining on to the floor,
I gaze at the intermittent lights that signal change, year on year,
the enormous scenarios of scarcity,
the useless weeds of this life.
Quiet in my stone I lick my dung-beetle's wounds,
the cud of the days' waste,
I chew my impotence and the hard drip of time,
a broken foot and the signal for flight.
Like a bug with nowhere to run I grieve.

¶

Contra sí mismo el cuerpo se revuelve,
cumple sus mil milímetros de pan,
migajas esparcidas, mendrugos,
se cuece en cada axila, huele,
cae ruminoso por el vientre, bocas,
pan mojado del sexo, tinto de olores, rancio.
Crece hacia dios el cuerpo, se eleva,
moja la cama y el amor, el pan y el vino.
Andan alisios por el pecho, nadan azules en las manos, andan.
En la impiedad de la cintura vuelve a instaurarse el miedo,
hay que tornar al punto del dolor, hacerlo sueño,
dar en el acto de la huida, descontraer.
Ante mis ojos crece como un pasto su aliento,
la negra majestad dulce del sexo, su pubis atestado y sudoroso,
la esparcida presencia en que penetro.
Desde mi centro rompen los cristales errados, se aquietan.
Una disolución inmaterial hace a la carne carne,
la piedra se machaca y se areniza.
Entrar es acudir al propio centro, una sabiduría que se desliza.
Allí se enciende, se pierden telas y lunares.
Pan, pan, carne del vino los cuerpos sudan,
jur, jur, jarrón rimado de la especie.

¶

The body turns round upon itself,
attains its thousand millimetres of bread,
scattered crumbs, hard crusts,
it cooks in each armpit, smells,
falls ruminating through the belly, through mouths,
damp bread of sex, stained with odours, sour.
The body grows towards god, rises up,
makes damp the bed and love, the bread and the wine.
Trade winds pass over the chest, swim blue over the hands, pass.
Fear returns, re-establishes itself in the ungodliness of the waist,
you have to go back to the source of the pain, make it
    become dream,
pounce in the act of flight, decontract.
Its breath grows before my eyes like pasture,
sex's sweet black majesty, its crammed and sweaty pubis,
the open presence that I penetrate.
From my centre the wrong windows shatter, grow still.
An immaterial melting makes the flesh flesh,
stone is crushed, becoming sand.
To enter is to come to one's own centre, a flowing wisdom.
There fire catches, and subjects and blemishes are lost.
Bread, bread, wine's flesh, our bodies sweat,
hurr, hurr, the recurring harmony of the species.

IV

de **NUECES**

II

El lugar, una peña y unas cuevas.
Enfrente, este paisaje idílico con caballos y nueces,
y los olivos con sus puntas de plata.
Si el escribir no fuera este mercurio
que escurre por la imaginación
recogiéndose siempre, sin dejar huella.
Ya sólo miro el puente que se estira,
la golondrina columpiándose.
Oigo los grillos en el valle amargo y amarillo.

IV

En una esquina un peletero
se oculta en un portal.
En otra un tallador, delicado picapedrero,
cuelga un conejo de su puerta,
los ojos abiertos y las orejas erizadas,
el calor de la piel ovillando su muerte.
Cuando regreso,
cuelga ya desollado.
En lugar de la piel los ligamentos,
el cráneo es lo que brilla, no los ojos,
la sangre es un sudor por los pellejos,
el cuerpo la delgada maravilla de músculos y nervios.
Dentro, la cercanía del tomate y las hierbas,
el olor seductor del sacrificio,
el acto comunal,
salvajemente humano,
apetecible y cruel de la comida.

IV

from KERNELS

TUSCANIA

II

The setting, a cliff and some caves.
In the foreground, this idyllic landscape with horses and
    walnut trees,
and the olives with their silver blades.
If only writing were not this mercury
that slides over the imagination
always gathering itself together, never leaving a trace.
All I do is look at the bridge stretching away,
the swallows swinging to and fro.
I hear the crickets in the sour, yellow valley.

IV

On one corner a furrier
skulks beyond his doorway.
On another a stone-mason, a delicate carver of marble,
hangs a rabbit from his door,
eyes open and ears erect,
the fur's heat curling its death.
When I come back,
it hangs skinned.
In place of fur, ligaments,
the skull is what shines, not the eyes,
the blood is a sweat that oozes through skin,
the body the thin marvel of muscles and nerves.
Indoors, the proximity of tomato and herbs,
the enticing aroma of sacrifice,
the communal act,
savagely human,
appetising and cruel, that is food.

VI

Sobre el paisaje ya asentado, ya conocido,
pinta una golondrina su desacato.
Abajo de ella, que ya se fue y que ya regresa,
el pino sigue, la casa, el humo al fondo.
El campo que se acunaba lo segaron.
En otras épocas hubiera llevado varios días,
un ritmo más áspero y cansado.
Hoy el tractor pasó su espada intransigente,
intachable.
Un perro ladra, muchos perros.
La basílica de San Pedro a la derecha
es una naturaleza de Morandi:
dos cajas, una jarra, media esfera,
el ocre seco contra un azul de paja.
Unas figuras borroneadas pudren la historia,
llenan la densidad del paladar
o la pregunta incontestable siempre
de quien la mira inquieto,
detenido en el espejismo inenarrable.

VII

Cuando un gallo canta
es un gesto rotundo y entero,
un acto singular del día que empieza,
una coherencia incontestable
que nulifica la desbandada luz horizontal,
la adormilada y lenta neblina
y que da solidez al árbol y al caballo,
seguridad al silencio que lo rodea,
certezas al principio y al despertar.
Cuando un gallo canta está unificando al mundo.

VI

Over the long-settled, familiar landscape,
a swallow paints its disdain.
Beneath the bird, already gone and already back,
the pine, the house, the smoke in the background all endure.
The field that rocked itself to sleep
is mown.
Years ago this would have taken several days,
a harsher, weary rhythm.
Today the tractor went over it with its relentless, stainless blade.
A dog barks, several dogs.
The basilica of St. Peter on the right
is a still-life by Morandi:
two boxes, a pot, a hemisphere,
a dry ochre against a straw-thin blue.
Some scribbled figures vex the story,
satisfy the thickness of the palate
or the ever-unanswerable question
of one who stares at it anxiously,
arrested by this inexpressible mirage.

VII

When a cock crows
it is a round and complete movement,
a singular act of the day just beginning,
an undeniable coherence
that makes a zero of the disordered light on the horizon,
the slow and dozy drizzle,
and lends solidity to tree and horse,
safety to the silence that surrounds it,
certainty to beginning and awakening.
When a cock crows it is joining up the world.

PUERTO

La ciudad sabe a mar,
da campanazos de salitre,
mece los brazos largos de sus sauces,
lame los ateridos huesos de sus plátanos,
se escapa en una enmarañada deserción.
Mueve los pies frenética en el cielo,
baila en el viento y en el agua,
y zapatea sus choclos con la lluvia, tap, tap.
Corre desesperada de callejón en callejón,
huye como si fuera la misma niebla,
y se va a pique con todo su ruidero.
Y más abajo el alma humana, su humareda, su chimenea,
su montón de infiernillos y discordias,
sus mil pasos prendidos a cada día.
Un inmenso mar de luciérnagas,
el puerto,
sus hombres y mujeres.

PORT

The town has a tang of the sea,
its bells toll saltpetre,
it cradles the long arms of its willows,
it licks the numb bones of its plane trees,
it escapes in a tangled defection.
Wildly it waves its feet in the sky,
waltzes in the wind and the water,
and tap-dances in sturdy lace-ups with the rain, clack, clack.
It runs in desperation from alley to alley,
flees as though fog itself
and founders with all its clatter.
And down further, the human soul, its cloud of smoke, its
    chimney,
its stack of petty hells and discords,
its thousand footsteps clinging to each day.
A vast sea of fireflies,
the port
with its men and women.

Es el viento como una marejada verde,
el remolino de hojas y de ramas,
Un ahogo el vórtice inhumano de los plátanos,
el oleaje de luz despedazada,
la inanidad ausente en el retumbo de las ventanas,
un barco ebrio atravesando cada minúscula hoja verde,
cada rama arañada en el ansia de la tormenta,
un desarraigo lento y repetitivo que se mide con la miseria
	de las uñas,
las pústulas del árbol aferrado a sus últimos meñiscos,
rítmico catamarán, árbol de mar agudo,
desguanzado bajel en una desatendida infinitud,
hundido en medio de la calle,
exhalando en la playa de sus hojas.

STORM ON TOLLINGTON WAY

It's a wind like a green swell,
the whirlwind of leaves and branches,
the plane trees' inhuman vortex a drowning,
the surge of shredded light,
the void missing from the booming windows,
a drunken boat cutting across each tiny green leaf,
every branch raked in the storm's anguish,
a slow and repetitive uprooting that is measured in the
      weakness of the claws,
the sores of the tree moored to its furthest curves,
a throbbing catamaran, tree of the biting sea,
emaciated vessel in an infinity of neglect,
sunk in the middle of the street,
breathing its last on the beach of its leaves.

COLEBROOK ROW

Por la mañana, sobre la banca,
mojando el alma y los brazos y el cuello del cerezo,
deja caer su manto el pelo frío del otoño,
la densidad de cuerpo y pasto
en un silencio de luz anieblada.
No es que un jardín espere.
Crece hacia sí, guarda secretos,
se llena de agua hoy, cruje mañana,
se entumece y alaba guarecido.
Y en un árbol el gato genealógico
es majestad de todo esto.

COLEBROOK ROW

Mornings, over the bench,
bedewing soul, arms and neck of the cherry tree,
the cold pelt of autumn lets fall its cloak,
the density of body and grass
in a silence of misty light.
It's not that the garden is waiting.
It grows into itself, hugs close its secrets,
today gets waterlogged, tomorrow crackles,
grows numb and is glad to be sheltered.
And up in a tree the pedigree cat
is lord of all this.

Vibra en el agua el grito chato de un pato,
el chorro sucio y oxidado de una pared de ladrillos
que alguna vez fuera una fábrica:
    "manufacturers of paper,
    parcels, stationery boxes,
    postal tubes".
Continúan el gotear de trapo,
la pezuña pálida de la luna,
las plantas que cuelgan del abandono, las chimeneas.
Repiquetea el cielo plateado en las virutas del agua,
en el vientre del puente, en esta historia de traspatio.
Un pato de cuello verde da una vuelta,
desaparece como una sombra gris.
El cielo se abre iluminando el alma.

REGENT'S CANAL

The flat quack of a duck trembles in the water,
the filthy, rusty flow from a brick wall
that might once have been a factory:
   "manufacturers of paper,
   parcels, stationery boxes,
   postal tubes".
What endures is the slow drip of rags,
the moon's pale hoof,
the plants drooping out of all this neglect, the chimney-pots.
The silvery sky beats down on the steel wool of the water,
on the belly of the bridge, on this history of backyards.
A duck with a green neck does an about-turn,
disappears like a grey shadow.
The sky clears, flooding the spirit with light.

REVÓLVER

Las dos alas del mar abren sus sábanas y espuma,
baten sus aguas anchas de sedas y de ahogados,
de bramidos y cargas y tempestades,
piélagos y esteros,
la mezcla dura de lo que queremos y lo que tocamos.
Por la ventana se ve llegar la tormenta,
en un segundo todas las señas desaparecen.
Somos una recámara de oscuridad,
un revólver el orbe.
El mundo es noche y allí estamos adentro,
balas cargadas y expectantes.
Afuera hay un pesado oleaje como pasto anegado,
como una manta espesa este calor que nos encoba.
Con el día la luz hace del mar otra pujanza.
El rojo escurre del sol un universo.
Es una rosa de los vientos amartillada.
El agua es nuestra, las balas silban,
nosotros somos muescas de su amor.

REVOLVER

The two wings of the sea unfold their sheets and their foam,
beat their waters, broad with silks and the drowned,
with roarings and cargoes and storms,
deeps and tidelands,
the hard mix of what we want and what we experience.
Through the window the storm can be seen approaching,
in a second all signals vanish.
We are a chamber in darkness,
the globe a revolver.
The world is night and we are there inside it,
loaded and expectant bullets.
Outside there is a heavy swell like drowned pasture,
the heat like a thick blanket hatching us.
With morning the light makes of the sea renewed strength.
Red wrings from the sun a universe.
It is a rose cocked by the winds.
The water is ours, the bullets whistle,
we are like notches of its love.

SERPIENTE

Encerrada en el círculo lento de sus actos
se desenrosca azul y colorada y amarilla,
una hilera de anillos estropeados,
güichi, güichi, la tierra raspa, duele,
se incrusta granulenta en la morosidad del cuerpo.
Se arrastra, *güichi, güichi.*
Apenas mueve alguna rama,
hace correr un ras de polvo,
una línea del suelo.
Alzada queda del esplendor plano por un impulso cervical,
por una continuidad de mil argollas que avanzan,
por un esfuerzo contráctil y apretado.
Al mismo tiempo la punta de la cola,
el latigazo alerta,
la lengua como perro agazapada al piso.
Toda la fuerza y el enojo se untan al suelo,
se adentran,
se achatan tensos a su presa.
Güichi, güichi.

SNAKE

Locked in the slow circle of its actions
it uncoils blue and red and yellow,
damaged rings all gathered in a necklace,
güichi, güichi, the ground is scraping, hurting,
lodging grittily in the body's slowness.
Creeping forward, *güichi, güichi.*
Barely a blade of grass it flusters,
making dust run on the level,
a line upon the horizontal.
It stays reared above splendid groundwork through an
    impulse in the neck,
through a continuing of a thousand coils advancing,
through a tightened and contractile effort.
At the same time too the tail's tip,
whip-lash watchful,
tongue out flat like a dog, afraid of being trampled.
All that strength and anger chafe the ground beneath it,
going inwards,
flattening and tensing for its prey.
Güichi, güichi.

EL ESCRIBA

Aquel hombre se sienta a la ventana.
Al fondo brilla el campo de su infancia,
una canción de cuna, alguna broma.
La tarde es roja y lenta,
su memoria no es más que literaria.
Él se mira verse irse, sonreírse.
Piensa en un niño puestos los ojos en un faro,
mientras la madre lo hace y acicala
intermitente, interminablemente
(un cuadro de costumbre es una intimidad que se repite).
Las cosas se unen en trabajosas junturas y dolorosos sesgos.
Él reconoce allí sus trastos viejos, sus sombras,
el avasallamiento de los hechos y su solidaridad,
su quieta reciedumbre y su urdimbre,
y avanza a cada paso como si fuera previsto,
como si tanta herrumbre convocara y nombrara,
y hereda así canciones y plumas y galletas y calcetines,
las usurpa y se hace de ese dolor que es ya ajeno,
ajado, que ya es historia,
una mercadería,
un trasiego sin fin de opacidades y brillos,
santos objetos de segunda mano, cuentas de vidrio,
        chucherías,
polvo dorado su negocio de mercachifle.

THE SCRIBE

That man sits at the window.
Out there the countryside of his childhood shines,
a cradle song, some joke or other.
The evening is red and slow,
his memory is nothing but literary.
He watches himself see himself, go away, smile.
He thinks of a child whose eyes have been placed in a
    lighthouse,
while the mother makes him and polishes
intermittently, interminably
(a picturesque scene is usually an intimacy that is repeated).
Things become joined in toilsome couplings and painful twists.
He recognises there his old junk, his shadows,
the compliance of things and their solidarity,
their quiet toughness and their cunning,
and moves forward step by step as though it were foreseen,
as though so much rust should summon and name,
and thus inherit songs and feathers and biscuits and socks,
and usurp them and out of this pain that is already someone else's,
crushed, that is already ancient history, fit it for
merchandise,
an endless reshuffling of opacities and sparkles,
blessed second-hand objects, tales made of glass, knick-knacks,
gold dust his pedlar's trade.

EL ARTE DE FECAR

Cagar es un placer, desgañitarse
por el caño febril y terminar
sin prisa alguna que nos lleve a odiar.

Cagar es como el arte de escribir:
hay que pensarlo y darle el tiempo justo
para que todo salga bien robusto.

Dicen los eruditos que lo saben
que nadie puede cometer suicidio
después de ese preciso infanticidio

y que limpia de cuajo toda culpa
y que deja el espíritu en muy alta
esfera de perdón, limpio de falta.

También es cierto, habrá que concederlo,
que como hay seres para cielo y cloaca
existen modos miles de hacer caca:

desde la huida desapavorida
de la angustia inminente del diarreico
o el caprino cagar del fariseico

hasta el atoro del que no quisiera
deshacerse de nada y todo estriñe
porque piensa que el mundo lo constriñe.

La perfección en el cagar reside
(si residir se puede en este gesto
que es más etéreo cuanto más es nuestro),

en llegar preparado y salir justo
casi como un selservis del desecho,
un, dos, tres, otro esfuerzo, ya es un hecho.

THE LIMINATING ART

Shitting is a pleasure, to bawl
along the feverish pipe and then abate
without the haste that might lead us to hatred.

Shitting is like the art of writing:
you have to give it thought and just so long
for everything to come out good and strong.

Sages declare – and they should know –
that no one ever thinks of suicide
on the heels of that precise infanticide

and that it scours and rids you of all blame
and leaves the spirit in an exalted
sphere of clemency, and cleansed of fault.

It's also true, let's face it, that just as some
are bound for heaven, some for the scrap-
heap, there are a thousand ways of having a crap:

from diarrhoea's imminent distress
and fearful voiding of the bowels
or the hypocrite's small goatish crottels

to the tight spot of the man who cannot bear
to part with anything so holds it in
because he feels life has a hold of him.

Perfection, when it comes to shitting, dwells
(if dwell it can in such a function that is
more ethereal the more noisome it is)

in coming prepared and leaving when you should
as though at a self-service, but of waste,
one, two, three, another effort – finished.

Porque quedar a medias es horrible:
el cuerpo lo resiente y se te enchina,
tiembla, se raja, escalofría, rechina

y en el alma y el cuerpo del causante
y en el cuerpo y el alma del delito
es muy mala señal hacer poquito.

For getting stuck halfway is horrible:
the body resents it, coming out in goose-flesh,
trembles, falters, shivers, makes you gnash

your teeth, and in the body and soul of the offender
and in the body and soul of the offence
it's a very bad sign to manage no more than an ounce.

ROSARIO

En la humedad de mi lengua la espiral de la serpiente.
En la frontalidad del cuerpo una espiga y el agua.
En la esperanza de los ojos la irisación del mundo.
En la minuciosa consternación de mis piernas la delicadeza
    de una uña.
En el ano el baño zodiacal.
En los pies las toxinas y el dolor del águila.
En codos y rodillas cuatro agujas al viento.
En las manos un cáliz perecedero.
En la espalda la enredadera y la raíz.
En la cabeza una pesada lama.
En el sexo la densa multitud, la espesa sed, la palabra.
En cada uno de los nombres aquí encontrados
una simiente de luz y una pesadilla de dispersión.
En mí mismo una ola que revienta.

ROSARY

In the moistness of my tongue the coil of the snake.
In the forthrightness of the body an ear of wheat and water.
In the eye's hopefulness the iridescence of the world.
In the thorough dismay of my legs the delicacy of one nail.
In the anus the zodiac's bathing.
In the feet the toxins and the eagle's anguish.
In elbows and knees four compass needles to the wind.
In the hands a perishable chalice.
In the shoulder the creeper and the root.
In the head a heavy slab.
In the sex the dense crowd, thick thirst, speech.
In every one of the nouns encountered here
a seed of light and a nightmare of dispersal.
In my own self a wave that breaks.

LUSTRAL

La cuchilla de agua de la luna
en esta noche, inmerecidamente.
Pega el silencio entre las manchas de los árboles,
capas oscuras, vetas de lava iluminadas.
Adentro, en una esquina,
un manojo podrido de magnolias
blancas, torcidas. Adentro el baño lustral,
afuera cables y ruidos rotos y los pájaros.
El columpio lunar, la rajadura de la luna, la uña de plata.
Salgo por esta noche hasta tu cuerpo.
Levanto el cáliz de tu carne, caigo
sobre tu espalda manantial, abro
tus piernas y las alas mojadas,
la lengua cierta,
el calamar, el agua vaginal.
Llevo las manos por tu espalda azul,
la grupa altiva, grabo
el recorrido de tu cuerpo,
el beso de la nuca, alzo
la menta amor de tus caderas,
ando
a cuatro patas por tu cuerpo, luna, te cabalgo,
luna,
te cabalgo,
mojada mantarraya
manto de Dios,
montuna.
Yo te monto.

LUSTRAL

The moon's watery knife
in this night, undeservedly.
It strikes silence between the patches of the trees,
dark cloaks, veins of lit lava.
Within, in one corner,
a withered clump of white, twisted
magnolias. Within, this outpouring of light,
outside, cables and fractured sounds and the birds.
The moon's swing, sliver of moon, fingernail of silver.
I go out into this night to your body.
I raise the chalice of your flesh, I fall
on your welling shoulder, I open
your legs and the wet wings,
the sure tongue,
the squid, the vaginal water.
I reach my hands to your blue shoulder,
the haughty rump, I engrave
the journey over your body,
the kiss on the nape of your neck, I lift
the beloved mint of your thighs,
I crawl on all fours across your body, moon, I ride you,
moon,
I ride you,
damp manta-ray,
mantle of God,
and mountainous.
I mount you.

DESPLAZAMIENTO DE LA COPA

Como la copa de cristal el alma,
los visos, brillos, bazas,
la balanza, la joya perceptiva,
la cadena de azules y de blancos.

Como el vino la copa de los cuerpos,
la fijeza dorada de la carne,
orfandad hecha savia, escurridiza
azúcar, escanciada y milagrosa.

Como el aire la copa derramada,
el vino hecho de luz, vuelco hacia arriba,
la gota transparente y siempre turbia,
el salar del amor y sus trasvases.

Como la palma la ciudad entera,
edificios, cortinas, ascensores,
escaleras del cuerpo, oscuridades,
puertas, frisos, umbrales, luces, bocas.

Como tu cuerpo el alma de la casa,
arrebujada, helada, calientita,
circulando en ti misma, apeñuscada,
azul hasta la sombra de este vino.

Como la copa la casa la palma,
como mi mano el vino hecho de aliento,
como su densidad brillante y pura,
entintada la casa hasta tu aroma.

Como mi cuerpo el vino, como la copa
el tuyo, como la casa el mío,
como la palma el tuyo, como tu boca
el vino, como el cristal entorno.

THE GLASS DISPLACED

Like a wine-glass, the soul,
the glints, the iridescence, tricks,
the comparison, the seeing jewel,
the sequence of blues and whites.

Like wine, the glass of our bodies,
the golden constancy of the flesh,
orphanhood become sap, sugar that slips
through the fingers, poured out, miraculous.

Like the air, the glass that is spilt,
the wine that's made of light, shooting upwards,
the drop that's transparent and always dark,
love's salt-lick and its shiftings.

Like the palm of the hand, the entire city,
buildings, curtains, lifts,
the body's stairways, darknesses,
doors, friezes, thresholds, lights, mouths.

Like your body, the spirit of the house,
wrapped up, frozen, perfectly warm,
moving around inside your shell, clamped,
blue to the very shadow of this wine.

Like the glass the house the palm,
like my hand this wine made of breath,
like its density pure and translucent,
the house wine-stained to the very scent of you.

Like my body the wine, like the glass
yours, like the house mine,
like the palm yours, like your mouth
the wine, like the glass entire again.

LOS PIES

Los pies se doblan, empequeñecen, huyen,
curvan su miseria y su miedo en unas líneas
que son las de la mano y no lo son.
Los pies son extensiones de Dios
(por eso están abajo),
de allí su angustia, su volumen redondo, su desajuste.
Los pies son como crustáceos asustados.
Tan sensibles los pies.
Se doblan y apeñuscan al hacer el amor
como si ellos fueran sus sujetos.
Los pies, así, no están hechos ahora
para prenderse como avispas
a cada aguja,
a cada rama del alma que allí los haga.
Son más alas que pies,
chiquititos y frágiles y humanos.
Tan desconsiderados que los tenemos.

FEET

Feet clench, make themselves small, run away,
creasing their wretchedness and fear in lines
identical to those on our palms and different.
Feet are extensions of God
(which is why they are low down),
hence their distress, their rounded bulk, their lack of balance.
Feet are like startled crayfish.
Such vulnerable things, feet.
When they make love they clench and huddle together
as though they were their own subjects.
So feet are not made, then,
to cling, like wasps
to every pine-needle pin,
to every branch of the soul that makes them there.
They are more wings than feet,
tiny and fragile and human.
However much we overlook them.

ACOTAMIENTO

Si yo no creo en mí.
Si yo no creo para nada en mí.
Si yo no creo ni en las tres cuartas partes de mis letras,
mi nombre,
el pedregoso y apedreado nombre,
si yo no creo en mí, me digo.
Si al decir "aquí estoy"
me quiebro como luciérnaga de polvo,
me escurro como pan ensopado.
Si yo no creo en mí.
Si ante la duda asumo
por fiel de la balanza
el gordo dedo de la derrota,
si arrinconado, a capa y espada,
vuelvo la desmesura un susurro estentóreo
y la mirada una lustrosa esfera fría,
si a guturales bajo los escalones, abro las puertas,
miro los terregales que son bosques,
si a la opulenta
suavidad de tu cuerpo
doy sólo el carraspeo de los huesos, la carne inhóspita
y así construyo un articulado edificio de odio;
si a tus palabras les pongo piedras y a tus pasos hogueras,
si hago de todo un emasculado manoseo,
si apenas tiento ya enciendo los faroles del frío,
si a tus acciones vuelco la milimetría del fatuo,
si erizo de instrucciones para no navegar el largo mar del alma,
si aminorado multiplico el desasosiego y el turbio andar,
si todas estas cosas han hecho de mí y de ti una calcinada
    impiedad,
si a mí me debes el aparejamiento y la decena trágica,
las gotas de mercurio y la ruindad.
Ante todo esto no puedo menos que decirlo y hacerlo
y dar en el sonoro pozo de mis propias paredes
y levantar el hacia y el hasta dónde

It's just that I don't believe in myself.
That I don't believe in myself at all.
In fact I don't even believe in three quarters of the letters
that make up my name,
that peters out in petrification,
because I don't believe in myself, I tell myself.
If, when I say "here I am",
I shatter like a glow-worm made of dust,
I ooze like bread dipped in gravy.
The fact is, I do not believe in myself.
For in the face of doubt I confuse
the needle on the scales
with the heavy finger of defeat,
for cornered, with cloak and dagger,
I turn lack of proportion to a bellowing whisper
and my expression into a cold and glittering globe,
for with gutturals I come down the steps, open the doors,
see expanses of dusty ground which are woods,
for I endow the opulent
softness of your body
with nothing but the rasping of my bones, with my
    inhospitable flesh
and so construct an articulated edifice of hate;
for I encumber your words with stones, your feet with fires,
for I turn everything into an emasculated pawing,
for the moment I touch you I light the lamps of coldness,
for I pour over what you do the precise calculations of the inane,
for I bristle with instructions on how not to navigate the broad
    sea of the soul,
for in my diminished state I multiply disquiet and restless pacing,
for all these things have made of me and of you a piece of
    blackened ungodliness,
for it is to me that you owe the gear and Gallipoli,
the drops of mercury and the shabbiness.
In the face of all this the least I can do is to say it and do it
and to fall into the echoing well of my own walls
and to raise the *towards* and the *as far as*

y levantar el cuerpo y el otro pie
y levantar las manos
y levantarme yo en mis propias andas
y decirlo.
Para que veas,
para que vea.

and raise my body and the other foot
and raise my hands
and to raise myself up from my own bier
and say it.
So that you may see,
so that I may see.

V

de RONDA DEL MIG

GOLONDRINAS

Enganchadas al cable como pinzas de ropa,
gaviotas de madera diminutas,
ágiles y minúsculas contra la brutalidad del azul,
fijas al mediodía cayendo una tras otra,
moviendo ropas, brazos, sonrisas,
el pecho blanco, la capucha negra,
las alas afiladas y en lista, mínima agitación.
Hasta que vuelan todas excepto una,
que se plantó un momento y arañó el regreso,
como una ligerísima despedida,
axila de golpe la mañana.
Quedan los cables, el cielo en abandono intenso,
como una boda de domingo de pueblo,
después nada.

V

from RONDA DEL MIG

SWALLOWS

Pinned to the wire like clothes-pegs,
diminutive seagulls made of wood,
lithe and tiny in the brutal force of the blue,
motionless at noon, dropping one after another,
setting in motion clothes, arms, smiles,
with white breasts and black caps, streamlined
wings and in single file, with minimal fuss.
Until all have flown but one,
that perched for a moment and clung to its return,
as though to sketch the lightest of goodbyes,
with morning suddenly an armpit.
The wires remain, the sky never so empty,
like a village wedding on a Sunday,
then nothing.

JARDÍN DE RODÍN

Como agua desierta
baja hacia las hierbas el caracol,
una mancha arborescente y fosfórica.
Pequeños pigmentos en la humedad revuelta,
por los lentos surcos del lodo,
en las membranas de la sombra.
Se pega a la pared buscando alivio,
paz en las baldosas, saliva en el dorso de la fuente.
Respira por el opresivo canal
entre hojas rugosas y astringencias.
Pegajoso se unta a su propio pasmo,
se deja ir con los gatos que ondulan,
maúllan hacia sus dársenas.
Fragilísimo el dardo y el redondel,
las machucadas flores dragadas.
Oye el chasqueo del agua,
el cuajar de las matas y su percutir,
el estigma y la sed violenta.
Paciencia, paciencia, petición de principio,
la marca del esclavo para siempre.
Prisionero en su asfixia,
las antenitas ágiles dispuestas,
deja una sal de baba, su senda.
Nada pasa entonces si se quiebra.
El agua corre y llena su propio ahogo.
Pasa y despoja.

RODIN'S GARDEN

Like water in the desert
the snail slips down towards grass,
a branching, phosphorescent stain.
Tiny pigments in the turned-over dampness,
along the mud's slow furrows,
in the webs of shade.
It sticks to the wall seeking relief,
respite on the paving-stones, spittle on the back of the
    fountain.
It goes breathing along the difficult channel
between rough leaves and astringencies.
Stickily it glues itself to its own fright,
it lets itself go with the swaying cats
who mew their way into harbour.
Utterly fragile, that dart and circling,
the bruised flowers it has dredged.
It hears water failing,
how vegetation hardens and rattles,
opprobrium and raging thirst.
Patience, patience, plea of origin,
the mark of the eternal slave.
Imprisoned in its stiflement,
the tiny, nimble horns alert,
it leaves a salty dribble, its trail.
Then goes nowhere if its shell is broken.
Water flows and fills it full to drowning.
Passing and plundering.

Como hojas de viento sorprendidas en ráfaga
se desprenden del grupo compacto,
un niño, dos, cada vez más,
levantan en vuelo para encrespar la calle,
soplados hacia sí, impelidos a unirse,
deshaciendo el grupo en el que estaban,
buscándolo de nuevo, conformándose.
Un imán los aleja y los reúne,
los dispersa primero hacia la calle,
los vuelve a congregar. Es muy extraña
esa manera de llenarse, hacerse ser.
Como si no supieran quiénes son sin seguimiento.
Se buscan, se tocan, se apelmazan.
Nada se da de golpe sino en un desafío
que los impide de uno en uno.
Hay dos o tres que ya han cruzado,
dos o tres más que empiezan a desprenderse,
hasta que, como si se expandiera el motivo,
el bucle se despega, vuela, se asimila,
cruza la calle en masa. Queda
un aliento, una suavidad que mece,
que acompaña a los rezagados, que los hace
ver que allá no están, que ya no están, que el grupo
está del otro lado. Todo
con una naturalidad de viento amable,
sin violencia, como en ciclo,
masa compacta nuevamente
al fin, tras movimiento, apaciguados.

Like leaves of wind surprised in a sudden gust
they peel away from the dense huddle,
one child, two, then several, more,
they take flight and ruffle up the street,
blown towards each other, impelled into merging,
unravelling the group they were in,
seeking it out again, finding their place.
A magnet drives them apart and tugs them back,
it scatters them first towards the street,
then brings them together once more. It's very strange
the way they fill out, make themselves be.
As though they don't know who they are unless pursued.
They chase each other, touching, colliding.
There's no giving way, except in a challenge
that blocks them one by one.
There are two or three who have already crossed over,
two or three more who are starting to break away,
until, as if the motive were spreading,
the curl escapes, flies free, tucks itself in,
and they cross the street *en masse*. A breath
of air lingers, a gentleness that rocks,
that wraps itself round the stragglers, making them
see that they're not there, they're not there yet, that the group
is on the other side. All
as natural as a kindly wind,
without violence, like a pattern,
a compact group once more
finally, after motion, calm and still.

CALA DE AIGUAFREDA

Al fondo del acantilado se amontonan,
macizas y grumosas,
las rocas que han ido cayendo,
barridas sin llegar hasta el mar
que muge y humea y rompe más abajo.
Dentro de miles de años,
me dices desde lo alto del camino de ronda,
eso será todo arena.
Miramos el nicho del mar
y como si el punto de foco se ampliara
o de repente se trastocara todo,
empequeñecimos infinitesimales
y vimos casi por dentro las enormes rocas.
A pie de playa contemplábamos
el movimiento granular de la arena,
los fragmentos de patas y caparazones de crustáceos
y nos guarecimos en cualquiera de esos guijarros.
Al disminuir tocamos en la rugosidad del guijarro,
un muro del que la arenisca se desprende,
nuestro propio contorno.
Fallas y grietas del mineral acumulado, eso somos.
En el cielo empezaron a vislumbrarse
las pajas de sombras y las vetas del gris.
Al respirar volvieron a aparecer los pinos,
el corte de la costa, el camino.

THE COVE AT AIGUAFREDA

They pile up at the foot of the cliff,
solid and lumpen,
these rocks that keep falling away,
landslides that never quite reach the sea
that bellows and fumes and breaks further down.
Thousands of years from now,
you tell me from our vantage-point on the curving path,
all this will be sand.
We look at this inlet of sea
and as though our perspective widened
or everything were suddenly topsy-turvy,
we became infinitesimally small
and could see almost inside these huge rocks.
Standing on the beach we considered
the sand's grainy motion,
the fragments of claws and crustacean shells
and we sheltered in one or other of those pebbles.
Shrinking, we came up against the pebble's roughness,
a wall from which the sandstone's rubbed away,
the outline of ourselves.
Faults and fissures of mineral accretions, that's what we are.
In the sky there began to be glimpses
of wispy shadows and seams of grey.
With our breathing the pines too came back,
the line of the coast against the sky, the path.

EN CAPILLA

Se incrusta la luz poro por poro,
tiñe los muros interiores,
mancha la oscuridad y la ilumina.
Como lengua porosa
deja una marea azul y bermeja,
una capa fina de luminosidad aplacada,
un envoltorio de polvo teñido.
Cascada de agua y sangre,
una placenta el púlpito,
piedra y hueco de amor
en donde crece quien va a nacer.
Por el vendaval cae la estirpe,
se redondea su calado,
piedra tras piedra,
fuente en la oscuridad.
Hacia abajo añiles granates,
por atriles y bancos hasta el altar,
apacible fuego el vitral.
Mi hijo y yo lo vemos de la mano.
Despacio crece la vida.

INSIDE THE CHAPEL

Light is inlaid, pore by pore,
tingeing the inner walls,
staining the darkness and illuminating it.
Like a porous tongue
it leaves a blue and vermilion tide,
a thin cloak of calm brilliance,
a caul of coloured dust.
Tumbling force of water and blood,
the pulpit a placenta,
stony hollow of love
in which the one who will be born is growing.
With the rainstorm comes the bloodline,
flood that swells, grows rich,
stone after stone,
wellspring in the darkness.
Down towards indigos and garnets,
past lecterns and benches to the altar,
the stained glass a soft fire.
My son and I see it with our hands.
Life is a slow growing.

PEDRO SERRANO has published five collections of poems: *El miedo* (Fear, México El Tucán de Virginia, 1986); *Ignorancia* (Ignorance, México El Equilibrista, 1994); *Tres poemas* (Three Poems, Caracas Pequeña Venecia, 2000); *Turba* (Peat, Ediciones sin Nombre, Mexico, 2005); and *Desplazamientos* (Displacements, Editorial Candaya – Candaya Poesia 5, 2007). His latest collection of poems, *Nueces* was published in 2009 and a study on T. S. Eliot and Octavio Paz, *La contrucción del poeta moderno: T. S. Eliot & Octavio Paz* was published by UNAM / Conaculta in 2011.

With Carlos López Beltrán, Pedro edited and translated the groundbreaking anthology *La generación del cordero: Antología de la poesía actual en las Islas Británicas* (The Lamb Generation, Trilce, 2000) which brought together translations of thirty contemporary British poets. His libretto for the opera *Marimbas de l'Exile / El Norte en Veracruz* was first staged in Besançon, France in January 2000 and then travelled to Paris and Mexico. He has also translated Shakespeare's *King John* into Spanish.

Many of his poems have been translated into English and have been published in *Modern Poetry in Translation, Verse, Sirena, The Rialto, The Red Wheelbarrow* and *Nimrod Internacional Journal*. He has been also included in the anthologies *Reversible Monuments* (Copper Canyon, 2002) and *Connecting Lines* (Sarabande Books, 2006).

Pedro Serrano was awarded a Guggenheim Poetry Fellowship in 2007. He teaches in the Faculty of Philosophy and Letters at the National Autonomous University of Mexico (UNAM) in Mexico City. He is editor of UNAM's highly-regarded poetry website, Periódico de Poesía.

ANNA CROWE, born in Plymouth in 1945, is a poet and translator and the author of four poetry collections in English: *Figure in a Landscape* (2010), a Poetry Book Society Choice which was translated into Catalan and published in a bilingual edition as *Paisatge amb figura* (Ensiola, 2011) and which also received the Callum MacDonald Memorial Award in 2011; *Skating Out of the House* (1997), *A Secret History of Rhubarb* (2006), *Punk with Dulcimer* (2006); one in Spanish / English bilingual edition: *L'ànima del teixidor* (2000); and one in Catalan: *Punk con salterio,* translated by Joan Margarit (2008). She has translated three of Joan Margarit's collections: *Tugs in the Fog* (Bloodaxe, 2006, a Poetry Book Society Recommended Translation); *Barcelona, amor final* (2007, Catalan / Castilian / English trilingual edition); *Strangely Happy* (Bloodaxe, 2011). She has also translated Anna Aguilar-Amat's *Música i escorbut* (Blesok, 2006); with Iolanda Pelegrí, an anthology of Catalan poetry, *Miralls d'aigua* (Light Off Water, Scottish Poetry Library / Carcanet Press, 2006); and, for Arc Publications *Six Catalan Poets* edited by Pere Ballart (2013).

Along with several other writers, she was a founder member of StAnza, the Scottish international poetry festival, and was artistic director during its first seven years. She has twice won the Peterloo Open Poetry competition, and in 2005 won a travelling scholarship from the Society of Authors.

W. N. Herbert was born in Dundee, and educated at Brasenose College, Oxford, where he published his DPhil thesis (*To Circumjack MacDiarmid*, OUP, 1992). He has published seven volumes of poetry and four pamphlets, and he is widely anthologised.

His first full collection, *The Testament of the Reverend Thomas Dick,* appeared from Arc in 1994. His last five collections, with Bloodaxe Books, have won numerous accolades. He has been shortlisted twice for the T. S. Eliot Prize and twice for the Saltire. He has gained three Poetry Book Society Recommendations, and won three Scottish Arts Council Awards. In 2000 he edited the bestselling anthology *Strong Words: Modern Poets on Modern Poetry* with Matthew Hollis.

Bill Herbert is currently Professor of Poetry and Creative Writing at the University of Newcastle-upon-Tyne.

Also available in the Arc Publications
'VISIBLE POETS' SERIES (Series Editor: Jean Boase-Beier)

No. 1 – MIKLÓS RADNÓTI (Hungary)
Camp Notebook
Translated by Francis Jones, introduced by George Szirtes

No. 2 – BARTOLO CATTAFI (Italy)
Anthracite
Translated by Brian Cole, introduced by Peter Dale
(Poetry Book Society Recommended Translation)

No. 3 – MICHAEL STRUNGE (Denmark)
A Virgin from a Chilly Decade
Translated by Bente Elsworth, introduced by John Fletcher

No. 4 – TADEUSZ RÓZEWICZ (Poland)
recycling
Translated by Barbara Bogoczek (Plebanek) & Tony Howard,
introduced by Adam Czerniawski

No. 5 – CLAUDE DE BURINE (France)
Words Have Frozen Over
Translated by Martin Sorrell, introduced by Susan Wicks

No. 6 – CEVAT ÇAPAN (Turkey)
Where Are You, Susie Petschek?
Translated by Cevat Çapan & Michael Hulse,
introduced by A. S. Byatt

No. 7 – JEAN CASSOU (France)
33 Sonnets of the Resistance
With an original introduction by Louis Aragon
Translated by Timothy Adès, introduced by Alistair Elliot

No. 8 – ARJEN DUINKER (Holland)
The Sublime Song of a Maybe
Translated by Willem Groenewegen, introduced by Jeffrey Wainwright

No. 9 – MILA HAUGOVÁ (Slovakia)
Scent of the Unseen
Translated by James & Viera Sutherland-Smith,
introduced by Fiona Sampson

No. 10 – ERNST MEISTER (Germany)
Between Nothing and Nothing
Translated by Jean Boase-Beier, introduced by John Hartley Williams

No. 33 – LEV LOSEFF (Russia)
As I Said
Translated by G.S. Smith, introduced by Barry P. Scherr

No. 34 – ANTONIO MOURA (Brazil)
Silence River
Translated by Stefan Tobler, introduced by David Treece

No. 35 – Birhan Keskin (Turkey)
& Silk & Love & Flame
Translated by George Messo, introduced by Amanda Dalton

No. 36 – Cheran (Sri Lanka)
In a Time of Burning
Translated by Lakshmi Holmström, introduced by Sascha Ebeling